Trust in God...
It's In His Hands

By Mike Sanders

Previous CAP books include:

- Faces of Poverty, 2002

- For Everything there is a Season, 2001

- Promise of Charity...Let Love Guide the Way, 2000

- Promise of Hope...Fear Not, I Am With You Always, 1999

- Promise of Faith...With Christ We Can Do All Things, 1998

- A Time of Crisis...A Time for Christ, 1997

- A Family of My Own...The Dream I Thought
  I Missed, 1996

- Pilgrimage of a Country Preacher...A Journey
  to the Holy Land of Appalachia, 1995

- Frontier of the Heart...The Search for Heroes in Appalachia,
  1994

- Called to the Mountains...The Autobiography of Father
  Ralph W. Beiting, 1993

- Dreams of Faith, 1992

- Promises to Keep...A Vision for Appalachia, 1991

- Appalachia...A Special Place...A Bridge of Hope, 1990*

- God Can Move Mountains, 1989*

* No longer available

This book is dedicated to my wife, Jackie, my children and their families for bringing me such happiness in life.

Table of Contents

Introduction   5

Chapter I   9

Chapter II   18

Chapter III   28

Chapter IV   43

Chapter V   57

Chapter VI   73

Chapter VII   89

Special thanks to the following people:

Front Cover drawing courtesy of Lewis Newman,
*   David Arts and Crafts*
Majestic photos provided by Pete Wolford
Majestic church photo provided by Ruby Dotson

Introduction

This book is written to explain, as much as possible, Mike Sanders getting to this plateau in his life, and how family, friends and CAP have been instrumental in helping his faith in God to grow. Mike shares with us how his faith has brought contentment, happiness and has provided him with armor to withstand the tricks of the devil.

When asked to write the introduction to this book the first thought that came to mind was, there are several people who know Mike Sanders better than I. Then I asked myself the question, "Is there anyone I know whose life has been more of an influence to me, or whose life has been a greater example for Christ than Mike Sanders?" I have admired Mike since the first day I came to work with CAP, some twelve years ago. But I suppose the last two years he has been an example of what it means to trust in the Lord. As Mike and Jackie, his wife and his three children have faced the trials, the triumphs and the disappointments of dealing with a disease that is life threatening, Mike has emerged as a spiritual leader.

In this book you will see how Mike, raised in a small rural town in Pike county by loving parents, served his country in the armed forces, began a family of his own, and worked at several different jobs to support them uses his faith as a witness for Christ throughout his battle with cancer.

The Christian Appalachian Project has played a major role in helping Mike achieve his goal in life to honor the words of our Lord recorded in Matthew chapter 25. It is there that Jesus said when you feed those who are hungry, give them drink, show hospitality, visit the sick and those imprisoned, that we have in essence served Him. It is here, in the daily administration of his duties as President of CAP that we, who are fortunate, not only see Mike talking the talk, but also walking the walk.

Several years ago I preached a sermon entitled "Salvation — God's Greatest Gift!" In that message I pointed out that salvation was God's greatest gift because:

God thought it
Jesus bought it
The Holy Spirit brought it
The Apostles taught it
The devil fought it
I caught it

For years we at CAP have been blessed with a leader who caught the salvation that God offered and lives a life that has inspired those who know him and work with him.

I, along with my colleagues am indebted to Mike Sanders for the way he has affected each of us with his close walk with his Lord. The greatest testimony that one can give, is when we as followers of Christ, live our lives in such a way that we influence those we walk this earthly journey with. It is my prayer, while you read this book, you will experience some of the excitement that has buoyed Mike as a Christian, as he becomes the individual God intended him to be when He created him.

Richard Ginn
CAP Chaplain

CHAPTER I

I will lift up mine eyes to the hills,
from whence cometh my help.

Psalms 121:1

I grew up in the hills of Appalachia, in a small Eastern Kentucky coal town called Majestic. As a boy growing up, I thought our town was the best place in the world.

I have seen and experienced many different parts of the world, including the war in Vietnam, but my heart never left the land that I call home. I lift up these beautiful mountains and the people here daily in prayer and will never again leave.

As a man, the mountains, the streams, the people have a greater and deeper meaning for me. I know now that the same feelings of beauty and home are present within the hearts of many who experienced life in the coal camps of Appalachia. That same sense of pride and home is still here today. It is as strong as it was when I was a boy. The hard times are still here and all that many have ever known.

If you ever lived in a coal town, you know of the hardships; the friendships and the faith that could only be found among the families that live in the rugged but beautiful mountains. Our town was no different. The houses were side-by-side and all looked alike. Everyone knew everyone and looked out for each other. Neighbors were like family and families were close and always there for each other.

Majestic was a typical coal camp. If I lean back and get quiet, I can still picture my life there, just as though it were yesterday. I can still hear the squeaking of the wheels of the coal trucks as they carried massive loads of coal down the mountains. I can smell the dust and see the faces and clothes, black from the days work, with only lips and eyes that came close to resembling those that went into the mine during the early morning hours. The hardhats, boots, and lunch pails were all part of the daily pilgrimage to and from the mine.

My Dad was one of those men. He worked hard to support his family and to provide a life for us. A life that was not filled with material things, but a life that gave us what was important; love, a sense of value and my faith.

I realize today that it was a hard life, with many tough times. We were poor, but

Majestic Colleries Miners

I know that I had what was important: a loving family.

There has been a great deal of changes in mining since the early days. Machines now take the places of men. They're digging more coal than they ever did, but lots of the work that was done by hand forty years ago is done by machines now. I've heard it said that one man, using the latest technology, could dig as much coal now as 10 men did when my dad was in the mines. Today, the jobs in the mines are few and many people have moved to find work elsewhere.

Majestic has suffered greatly through the years as the coal companies have come and gone. People of the area have found it hard to feed their families and keep their homes. Jobs are few and the numbers of jobless are high.

My Dad retired as a miner and my family still lives in Majestic. The area will always be home to Mom, Dad, my sister and me.

I was diagnosed with colon cancer in July 2000. I underwent surgery and found that it had spread to my lymph nodes. I was treated with chemotherapy for 6 months. I then learned that the cancer had spread to my liver. I had surgery and another round of chemotherapy. An additional diagnosis required another treatment and another round of chemotherapy. Months of treatment, including an experimental trial, have had good results.

The past two years have been very difficult for my family and I think that must be true with all illnesses; those that care for you feel the pain.

However, God gives us some of our greatest rewards during our times of greatest need. During my period of recuperation after liver surgery, my first grandson, Jacob was born. That little guy brought me so much pleasure I really didn't have time to think about myself.

Then, during another round of treatment, my granddaughter, Lauren, was born. Again, I was able to focus on the miracle of life and the happiness these babies have brought into our family. I truly believe that a combination of great nursing from my wife of 32 years, Jackie, the love of my entire family and prayer, a lot of prayer from a lot of people, are responsible for the good news I've gotten recently from my doctors.

I have spent the last two years beginning my day and ending my day in prayer; prayers for all of those who mean so much to me. I feel so blessed because each time I was told that the cancer had come back, God found a way to guide me through the times of pain. He blessed me with a wife who has cared for me as none other, children who have been there, and two wonderful grandchildren who have brought so much joy into my life. So many caring people have surrounded me. I do feel that I am where I am today, no evidence of cancer at this time, because I have had so many people pray for me and because of my strong belief that God will care for me.

My wife has always had such faith and trust in God. She has always been the one to bring Christ into our daily lives. When we found I had cancer, the thing that stands out most in my mind is something that Jackie said to me, she said, " trust in God, it's in his hands". Each day I trust in God, and I have placed my life in his hands.

I try each day to make someone's life better, I love to joke and I think there is nothing greater than to see someone laugh and feel joy. It brings with it a healing power.

I have found that we never have to suffer alone; God is with us every step of the way. There were many times during the treatments that I asked him for help. He would always ease the pain.

I think of the pain Jesus suffered to give us a chance for life and salvation. My pain was so small compared to His.

I have tried to not spend time worrying about my cancer. I have chosen to spend my time enjoying every minute of each day and treasuring those around me. I have a wonderful family, many friends, and I spend each working day involved in helping those people in Appalachia who mean the world to me.

Something else I know for sure has contributed to my healing is the work I do as president of the Christian Appalachian Project. When I began working here, God surely knew even then how the organization would impact my life and my survival of cancer. The people I work with at CAP have become a second family, and my years of working with them has been yet another blessing in my life. I was in my early thirties when I began to work for CAP, and in those nearly 20 years, I can see that CAP has given my life a real purpose, and I've grown in many ways, including spiritually.

I find strength in serving others and I feel Christ working through us in the work we do at CAP every day. I look forward to going to work; it takes my mind off my cancer.

In the early 80's I met Monsignor Ralph Beiting. He impressed me so much with his commitment to Appalachia and helping the poor of the area to have a better life. I was sold from day one and I began my journey with The Christian Appalachian Project. I have spent the years since helping others in an area that I love very much.

CHAPTER II

But lay up for yourselves treasurers in heaven, where neither moth nor rust doth corrupt, and where thieves do not break through nor steal: For where your treasure is, there will your heart be also.

Matthew 6:20, 21

In 1986, CAP started a program called Operation Sharing, one of my favorite programs because it does exactly what it says it's going to do — it shares.

It is a gift in kind program that helps families, churches, communities and other non-profit organizations throughout the 13 Appalachian states. If there is a disaster in the area Operation Sharing is there!

We provide many necessary supplies for clean up, and for recovery. We not only assist during the disaster, we also continue to offer assistance to the community as long as the help is needed. I spent many years heading up CAP's Operation Sharing and was able to witness many lives helped through this program.

In the spring of 2002, the community of Majestic was faced with a challenge. It's a challenge the town has faced before many times. A heavy spring rain resulted in many inches of rain in a very short time and water poured down those mountains and overflowed the creeks and riverbeds in nothing flat. Flash flooding always catches communities off-guard. Many homes were damaged and some people lost everything.

When Hilman Dotson, a life-long school-mate and friend, now a magistrate in Majestic, said that help was desperately needed, Operation Sharing immediately responded. CAP delivered much needed supplies and goods to the Majestic community.

Through the years, CAP has received many donations through Operation Sharing; gifts from corporations, other nonprofits and individual donors, gifts from all over the country. We've always known we had good friends; people who wanted to reach out and help Appalachia as much as we did. From the very beginning, Operation Sharing called on folks to work together to help people who needed help.

A while back, we heard from a man who wanted to donate bicycles that he fixes. He takes bikes that kids have outgrown, repairs the chain, fixes or replaces the tires and rubs them down so they look as good as new. He knows that not many poor kids don't have bikes, so he wanted to give them

Majestic Colleries company store

to us for kids in our programs.

Through our outreach program, we learned of a family that really needed a boost. There were seven children in the family, and several months earlier, the mother had left the family. This type of thing happens often to families in the area. No money, no work, can cause so much stress on families.

We learned that one of the little boys in that family had cancer. The child's father was doing the best he could do, trying to get the child to his treatments, and take care of the others. CAP had been helping in many ways, but I don't think anything brought a bigger smile to the face of the boy and his father than one of the bikes. It was like Christmas.

Operation Sharing delivers hope with each truckload of goods that go out into the area. Today, well over 100 businesses and organizations make donations to Operation

Sharing. We still get loads and loads of books just as we did with our first shipment years ago. But often we get lots of other things that help improve our programs and the programs of many organizations in the region.

County health departments have received an abundance of Operation Sharing items, and we hear that some of their favorite things are the dental hygiene items. Educators teach classes at the local elementary schools about the importance of kids taking good care of their teeth and gums. After a demonstration of good brushing and flossing, everyone receives a toothbrush.

Some donations can have specific uses, and we try to get them where they can be used best. Donations of safety equipment distributed to rural fire departments, such as Bell County in the southeast part of Kentucky, can save lives. When we received thousands of dollars worth of this equipment, volunteer fire fighters helped us sort it and deliver it to other departments. In these small counties without a very big tax base, departments received equipment that they otherwise would have never had. "Operation Sharing is one of the best things that ever happened to Bell County," said Larry Browning, chief of the volunteer fire department. In two years, the department received over $150,000 worth of equipment that would have never been available otherwise.

The worth of these donations goes beyond their monetary value to the good that we do with the materials we receive from all over the country. We've gotten thank you notes from teachers and children; teachers tell of the look in the eyes of a child who receive a book to take home. Some of these kids have never had a book of their own before.

Donations of building supplies through Operation Sharing let us add another aspect to our home repair program by stretching resources. Our warehouse assistant director, Carol Parrett, tells me that CAP workers call often to learn what's in the warehouse or to ask director Johnny Thompson to keep an eye out for a certain item. The folks in our outreach program have used Operation Sharing building supplies to give the emergency home repair program a good start. With the use of Operation Sharing materials, they're able to give the materials directly to the homeowners who can make their own repairs with the help of friends and neighbors.

It was an exciting time when CAP got its first donation in 1986. Last year, Operation Sharing received about $58 million worth of in-kind donations. Of that, CAP programs used approximately $5 million worth of these goods; the balance was given to nearly 1500 organizations throughout the Appalachian region for use in schools, churches and grass roots relief programs.

I'm happy to report, too, that half of the

materials we receive each year come unsolicited because CAP has a reputation for making good use of donated materials. The other half is solicited, based on the needs of our programs and the needs of other programs we share with.

Carol says about 25 groups come to the warehouse every day to pick up items they can use from our donations. Old friends, new friends, even telephone numbers copied from the sides of commercial vehicles have all given our folks the leads they need to obtain materials Operation Sharing can distribute in Appalachia.

Storage space is expensive and corporations must get rid of materials they stored in the past. People like to make donations to Operation Sharing because we can pick up materials anywhere in the southeast, usually within a day or so, and people like to know that the materials they're giving will be going to good use. When people give to us, they know things won't be sold. There's no hidden profit gimmick; it's going to be distributed free and it's going to people in need.

The appearance of Operation Sharing can be deceiving. A warehouse full of materials that might include anything from pallets of insulation to boxes of cologne doesn't begin to tell the tale of the relationships that make Operation Sharing special.

These relationships stand today because of the friendships that have developed from working together. Our participants don't just load a truck and drive off. We take time to get to know one another, share a cup of coffee and show pictures of children and grandchildren.

If I were to describe Operation Sharing in terms of materials in the warehouses, that would only be partially accurate. The real story of Operation Sharing is in the relationships that have developed throughout the Appalachian region by organizations that are working together.

Working together like this reminds me a lot of growing up in Majestic. And just like those neighbors back in Majestic, they're more like family than friends.

CHAPTER III

The Lord is my light and my
salvation; whom shall I fear? The
Lord is the strength of my life, of
whom shall I be afraid?

Psalm 27:1

I have found great strength, not only through my faith, but also through my family. Both are a vital part of my life. Both have helped shape me as a person, a son, a brother, a husband, a father, and a man of God.

Life has been a great journey for me, beginning with my parents, who have given me so much through the years. They did without in order to provide for their children.

Our house was always open to family and friends, whether it was for a meal or just visiting. Sharing was part of our life. Not only sharing of food, but experiences and skills. I learned a great deal from my Uncle Claude who could build or make anything. Another person who influenced me greatly was Reverend Furrow, who has been at the same church for 47 years.

My Mom taught me many values displayed by example or by the actions taken when I didn't do as I was told. She was a hard worker, and fulfilled her duties to our family. I can still remember the rattling of the coal in the bucket as she shook the embers in the old coal stove to get our fire going in the morning. I can still remember the chill of the room and the touch of my foot to the cold floor.

Today, I feel so fortunate, because again, I have gone through tough times and my family has surrounded me, just as it did years ago as a child.

My sister and her husband mean so

much to me. I treasure my brother-in-law and think of him as a brother. Both my sister, Susie, and Steve have been there for me, just as they are daily for my parents in the twilight of their life.

I have been given many blessings in my 52 years of life, but the blessing that I hold dearest is the blessing of my wife, Jackie. She has always been there for our family and me. She has helped me find Christ through her own faith and devotion. Through our 32 years of marriage, I have found her to be a wonderful mother and the most caring wife a man could ever hope to find. She has been strong, when I was weak, she has been kind, when kindness was needed, and she has provided strong guidance and direction for our children. My struggle with cancer has been so hard on her, but she has never failed to do everything possible to ensure that I was given the best care.

A sense of family and faith is so important

to the people of Appalachia. My work at CAP has helped me witness that bond of family.

I had a brother who was born handicapped. My parents felt from the beginning that he was a blessing instead of a burden. We lost him when he was five, but his memory is forever part of our family.

It might seem funny to talk about the blessings of illness, but sometimes I really think that I have been blessed in the months that I've been battling cancer. This especially comes to my mind when I hear from an old friend I haven't talked to in a long time, folks that have called after they've heard I had cancer. They want to see how I'm doing, but thankfully, we get that out of the way in a hurry and turn to more pleasant topics.

We'll start talking about the old days growing up in Pike County, or days in the Army and swap stories about what we've been up to since the last time we talked. More than anything else, it makes me promise, at least to myself, to make a better effort to keep up with old friends.

When I hang up the phone, I often think back on all the people who were such an influence on me when I was growing up; like my Uncle Claude, my dad's brother. Like most of us in the mountains, Uncle Claude didn't own a lot of material things, but he could make just about anything with his hands.

My dad loved to fish and he asked his brother to help him build a boat. I got to help and I never had so much

Mike with his mother and father during his senior year of highschool

fun in my life. We went to the sawmill, picked up the rough lumber. My uncle drew up the plans, got out the tools, and together we built a boat.

I've seen bigger boats, and fancier boats, but never a boat that I took more pride in riding. It was 12 to 14 feet long, made with boat gunnels for the sides and straight boards for the bottom ends and seats. We stuffed rags in the cracks and dammed up the creek so we could sink the boat so the boards would swell together. After it was painted, we went fishing on the Tug River.

Needless to say, from Uncle Claude I learned to work with my hands, and I've come to love puttering around building things and fixing things. In fact, I fixed up a garage behind my house and when I have time, I love to work on classic cars and trucks. I've infected all three of my kids with that love, too, and they tell me that some of the best times we've ever spent together are the times we've been working in the garage. Even today, whenever my children break something, they say daddy can fix it. They give me too much credit.

Lately, I've used time in the garage to pray and reflect. And a couple of times, I've considered how much my life changed after I got involved with the Christian Appalachian Project. If you'd told me 25 years ago where I'd be and what I'd be doing today, I would never have believed it.

My relationship with CAP began when I was asked to take care of their cars. I said "sure," but somehow I knew I had just volunteered.

A couple of years later, when I was getting ready to sell my business, I pondered what I was going to do for the summer. I had intended to take some time off. We had a boat and lived near the lake and I was looking forward to doing some serious loafing and fishing before going to work in the mines. But God had other plans and Monsignor Beiting convinced me to volunteer my time with CAP that summer. I think it was the best summer of my life — it sure changed the rest of it.

At the end of the summer, I was offered a job with CAP for several thousand dollars a year less than I would have made in the mines. But I fell in love with CAP that summer, so the decision wasn't really that difficult. I know now, too, that it wasn't even in my hands — it was in God's hands.

Nearly twenty years later, I see clearly what prompted me to make such a change. I realize now that I was attracted to the spirituality of this organization and the people that made up this ministry. Majestic, where I had grown up, was a church-going community and I grew up around lots of ministers and preachers who had served their churches and congregations for many years.

But from CAP I've learned that while it's important to read the Gospel and preach the Gospel, it's even more important to live the Gospel.

From CAP I've learned that it's possible to pray all the time, not just when you're in church.

From CAP I've learned that we don't have to please the government, we don't have to please other organizations, and we don't even have to please ourselves. The only one we have to please is God, and when we're pleasing God, everything will work out for the best.

I think one thing that's made CAP as successful as it is, is the fact that we're an inter-denominational organization. When CAP was founded, it was important that everyone feel included in the organization's work and programs. We all love and worship the same God and it's important that we focus on the things that draw us together rather than things that separate us. It's important to remember that when we pray together, it's the most important work of all.

Our ministry at CAP reaches out to provide

the physical and spiritual needs of those suffering. I am surrounded daily by God's words and messages.

At 9:30 each morning, in a small but humble chapel, the employees of CAP, sometimes joined by those we help and local ministers and friends, come together to pray. It truly is the coming together of the children of God. I have seen all faiths present throughout the years. We all find a great deal of consolation each day as a different person leads us in our daily prayers. We share our sorrows, the illnesses of our friends and families, births and deaths, the tragedies of the world, and we answer many prayer requests from our distant family members, our donors who help us.

Chapel at CAP is my favorite time of the day. It is so special, because we all provide spiritual strength for each other. For me, it is the most productive time of the day. It is a daily reminder of the importance of God in our lives.

I've learned a lot about prayer, too, from the people in some of our programs. While we have programs that help people make long-term changes in their lives, some of our programs help people deal with immediate crisis — help with the rent, help with domestic violence, and help with heat or clothing. Inevitably, the people who come to us in times of crisis have learned to depend on God.

During my time with CAP, I've learned of the importance of community and group prayer. It's not a written policy, but every CAP meeting, whether it involves employees, board members or folks who participate in our programs, begins with prayer. In fact, I have found that I miss not beginning with prayer when I'm attending a civic meeting, for example, and usually quickly whisper for guidance in whatever matter we're discussing.

I remember one morning during Chapel a request was read from a man who had asked us for prayer. He had sent us a dime, and told us that the dime was all he had. He hoped that in some way it would help those in need. I thought how important that dime was to him and how blessed we were to receive it, because it was all he could give, all the extra he had.

There are many wonderful stories of faith and giving at CAP. It is faith that sustains our organization. It is our strength and our guidance; doing God's will every day, praying for his guidance as we find ways to relieve the pain and suffering of others.

Years ago when I first came to CAP, Monsignor Beiting bought CAP's first piece of property in a small town called Martin, in Floyd County. We were so excited; it was an old funeral home that had been owned by the Hall family.

It was located on Main Street and had been tied up in litigation for four years. No one thought that we had a chance of getting the property. Monsignor Beiting, our founder, continued to work on contacting the owners until finally they agreed to sell us the building! They not only sold us the building, they donated half of the money back to our organization.

We finally had a place to work. It was in bad condition so we began to work day and night repairing plumbing, roofs, floors and painting. We had plans for offices, a teen center and a maintenance area to keep our cars going.

We were ready to move in, when the area was hit by a major flood. Our building had several feet of water standing in all the newly finished rooms. We had exhausted all we had to get the building to where we had, and now, it was as bad as it was when we started. Everything was covered with mud. We had spent $25,000.00 on the building and never got to move in.

The area was devastated, as was our

building. Many people lost everything they had. After the water went down, we began the clean up. It was some of the hardest work I have ever done. It seemed that the more mud we shoveled, the more there was. The carpet was so laden with mud that we had to cut it into strips to carry it out. We were weeks doing the clean up.

I feel that God was watching over us, because, I ran into the gentleman who had sold us the building and was telling him about our devastation. He remarked that he had a policy on the building that was probably still in effect. He would check and get back to me. He did and we were able to get $25,000.00 and start again.

Every time we learn of a flood in Appalachia and CAP helps a community or family with flood relief, I'm reminded of the devastation that a flood can bring. I know of the loss and the pain that comes with losing your family possessions. I am so happy that we are able to provide relief for families when this act of nature occurs.

This story and so many more like it make me mindful that through poverty, flood, fire (we've had a few) and even cancer, "The Lord is the strength of my life; of whom should I be afraid?"

No matter what we do, no matter where we go, as long as we remember that it's all in God's hands, we'll never go wrong.

Devastation from floods in eastern Kentucky

CHAPTER IV

*Listen to me, you who pursue justice,
who seek the Lord.*

Isaiah 51:1

There have been mornings when I leave very early and drive deep into the mountains to monitor a program or meet with staff. I am always awed by the beauty of the mountains as I drive farther and farther, each mile winding along the mountain tops or down into the valleys.

The fog nestled over the valleys looks like a giant comforter. It is such a beautiful picture, that words cannot describe what one sees and feels. I have often wondered about creation and how perfect God's hand was when he created this area. I also wonder how it must have looked hundreds of years ago.

There are times when I remember words that tear at my heart:

"Just before dawn, the fog was thick and the dew was heavy on the mountain. With bruises and maybe broken bones from the nightlong fight, I gathered my children and left for the last time. I found refuge at CAP. CAP saved my life and probably the lives of my children."

Those words will always be with me, especially when I think of the abuse that happens every day in the mountains. These were the words of a wonderful lady that we were able to help.

Domestic violence is one of the saddest stories we have to tell in the mountains, and one of the most shameful. The pressures of isolation, poverty and unemployment weigh on many mountain people, but the majority of them bears up and does the best they can with what they have. Often times it's those that are loved the most that are lashed out at during times of violence and anger.

Barbara is an inspiration to many, she was able to gather the strength to take her children and leave what was familiar behind. With the help of CAP she was able to get an education and establish a new life for herself, a life as an educator, a life that would allow her to help others.

Our spousal abuse programs are able to provide for a short time, feelings of love and safety for many adults and children each year. To some it may seem like a last hope. It is hard to imagine what each of these victims have experienced: the hurt, the fear, the loneliness and the feeling of not being good enough. I am so thankful and proud of these programs that play such an important role in the lives of many.

Growing up, life was learning to overcome obstacles. They were not obstacles of abuse, but daily obstacles that life can sometimes

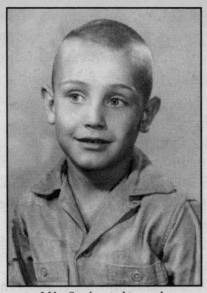
Mike Sanders in his youth

put in your way. I learned to have patience, to plan, and to work hard. That is what we do at CAP as an organization. We help people to overcome the obstacles of poverty one step at a time. Growing up and surviving in Appalachia is a challenge, especially if you do not have the resources necessary for survival.

Among the many things I've learned

during my cancer treatment, one stands out as the most important: Stay focused on your goals and never give up. I feel certain that through prayer and good medical treatment, I'll survive, and even come through stronger than ever.

Sometimes I feel like Satan hopes that I would blame God for my cancer. I know Satan is powerful, but as long as we keep our eyes on God, we render him weak. Instead of being discouraged, I see God helping me through these difficult times, through the pain and suffering. Whatever pain I might have is minor, compared to the pain that Christ suffered for all of us. Instead of turning away, cancer has helped me grow even closer to God.

Many people that I've met through CAP's programs live that way, too. They trust in God, moving determinedly past the obstacles set in the way. I'm touched by the efforts that moms and dads make to provide food and shelter for their children. Since welfare reform began in 1996, I've been impressed by the efforts that people have made to comply with the regulations for education and training. Many of these moms have gone from welfare to low paying jobs, and are still going to school so they'll be able to get better jobs. More than anything else, I can see that they never give up and they inspire me to live with the same attitude.

In the early days, we did not have the money to hire staff. I was the first staff person hired in the eastern area. We were able to get many volunteers from all over the country to come and help us. I was so impressed and touched by people who had no ties to the area, they simply wanted to give of themselves and help those less fortunate.

I had never met people like the CAP volunteers who have moved from their homes, many of them hundreds of miles away, to an area where they had no family or friends, to work at a job helping other people. These people became family to me and I treasure each memory and all the hard work we shared.

Monsignor Beiting used to say, " A tired volunteer is a happy volunteer." He was so right. We must have had the happiest volunteers in the world. In the early days and even today our volunteers are the backbone of our organization.

We think of our volunteer program as a stool with three legs, legs that represent prayer, community and service. Volunteers talk about sitting around late into the night, discussing what's most important, prayer, community or service? Before they turn off the lights, they'll agree that without one the other two would crumble.

The desire to serve is a common bond for volunteers and the easiest to talk about because it's tangible. Some people arrive with service already an important part of their lives. They've gone to school to be nurses or teachers. Others have clerical or business skills. The gifts they offer might be different, but for most, the motivation is the same. Church tradition and encouragement from family motivates many, which is also related to prayer and community.

Of these three elements, community is the most difficult to explain. Some volunteers say that they have developed ties that are closer than blood kin. They have a special bond that grows out of sharing many things, including chores, the bathroom, pain, joy and prayer.

Some of our volunteers come from this area. I remember one lady who wanted to help her community. Her name was Cleo Howell, a wonderful person who loved her family more than life. She served as my secretary for many of my earlier years at CAP. She was such a joy, so positive and always happy. She worked hard to help us set up our office and enjoyed every minute of the work. We later were able to employ her. I will never forget her work, her laughter, and her love for the people of the area. She loved CAP and was a good friend to many. She passed away a few years ago; I miss her and will never forget her.

For most CAP volunteers, the move to Appalachia is their first experience with a new culture and for some, it's the first time they have been away from home. For others, it's their first experience after college. Living with a group of people who are going through a similar experience makes what could be very difficult or even impossible, adventurous and joyful.

CAP Volunteer

This is where prayer and community really start to blend together, as the community becomes the presence of God to its individuals.

Volunteers say that at its worst, living with a group of adults who are searching, and in may cases, searching for the same thing, can be the most frustrating experience of a person's life. At its best, life in a caring, Christian community gives individuals the opportunity to see God in each other. They say that living in community gives them the responsibility—and the privilege—of reflecting God to others in their home, and even more importantly, to those they serve.

We've been blessed to have a few employees who have come to CAP after service in the Peace Corps, or other volunteer programs. From them we've learned that the motivation of volunteers is similar in different program and geographic locations.

Several years ago, our elderly program was managed by Susan Scott, who came to CAP after service in Sierra Leone with the Peace Corps. She had interesting insights to share about the willingness of volunteers to learn new things and acquire new skills. Many volunteers who have worked in the elderly program, for example, have become expert "quilters" from the time they've spent with quilting "mentors." Others who have worked in our child development programs have returned to college to get advanced degrees and are now some of the most accomplished professionals in the state in the field of early childhood education.

"Volunteering is a self-maturing process," Susan says. "It is a stage in our lives that we carry with us, though, because it has nurtured us. I think that the people we serve recognize this. Elderly people may not be aware of their powerful influence in our lives, but participants do recognize that our volunteer experience is a stage in our lives. Many volunteers have come into their lives and left just as abruptly. Yet they appreciate the arrival of the next volunteer. Why would a young person from New York want to come to Kentucky to visit an elderly person? It's hard to say, but they do not just do it, they revel in it and often savor it for the rest of their lives."

In the last few years, CAP has been on the receiving end of services from people who have decided to use their retirement years for volunteer work. Although we treasure the youthful enthusiasm of volunteers who give us those first years after college, we're equally grateful for the services of people who only have time and energy to contribute and the wisdom that comes with age and experience. Betty Laukhuf, for example, brought the experience of her 66 years to the elderly services program in McCreary County.

Volunteers at Workfest

An ordained minister in Restoration Fellowship Church, a Pentecostal faith based in the rural Midwest, Betty retired from factory work, and then took a job organizing social events for residents in a nursing home in Indiana. She loved her job, but a story in an old, dog-eared copy of The Mountain Spirit introduced her to the Christian Appalachian Project and our elderly services program. She found herself drawn to an advertisement about CAP's volunteer program, and before she knew it, she had called our 800 number and was working out the details for an interview with the volunteer department.

"God doesn't mess around," Betty says. "The message could not have been any plainer if He'd sent me a letter telling me to pack up my clothes and head for McCreary County."

Volunteers young and old say they believe that God has called them to work in the mountains of Appalachia and we believe that through our volunteers CAP is able to share the spirit of service throughout the United States. It's hard to quote exact numbers, but I'd say that hundreds of CAP volunteers have chosen to stay close to the mountains, starting a home and raising a family. Thousands, though, have returned to their homes throughout the United States and now share their talents in other places. The importance of prayer, community and service stays with CAP volunteers no matter where they go; through them, CAP influences communities far beyond the mountains of Appalachia.

CHAPTER V

Suffer the little children to come unto me, and forbid them not: for of such is the kingdom of God

Mark 10:14

Suffer the little children...these words are always with me as I witness the children of Appalachia. Children that struggle for survival each day. A struggle that is so great, that they think going hungry, being cold, and enduring abuse is a normal way of life. They are challenged daily. Challenged to find a better way. Challenged to dream.

My childhood in Appalachia was one of being challenged, being creative and enjoying life by making the best of what I had. We didn't have computers or any of the expensive toys that are available today.

We learned to use our minds and the resources of the mountains. With each season, we created our own fun and games. I often think that my life during the summer mirrored that of Huck Finn.

We would climb the mountains every summer and start building a log cabin. We worked hard gathering the limbs from small poplar trees, figuring how to place each limb, dreaming of how great it would be to have our own recluse.

Summers came and went, and we never finished one of those cabins, but the dreams of what could be were what meant the most and stayed with me.

We often cut the tops from old cars and tried to float them down the streams. We explored the old coal train tracks and built a buggy that we could ride on the tracks. We camped out by the river and ran trotlines all night. We rode ponies, swung on grape vines, made bows and arrows and pretended to be Roy Rogers, Hop-a-long Cassidy or the Cisco Kid.

As evening came and the quiet of the mountains brought a solitude that is hard to describe, I remember how things would wind down with only the occasional creaking of a porch swing. I remember the evening games of catching or just watching lightning bugs, the sound of the crickets and the hide and go seek games.

I loved the Appalachian summers, the days were long and life was simple. There was nothing that can compare to an early morning lying on a swing or on a porch, feeling the morning sun warm your face and body. Feeling so alive and safe.

Fall in the mountains always came too quickly. It meant school and new shoes; it brought radiant color that covered the mountains. The coal piles beside the houses grew larger with each load and the smoke began to curl from the chimneys signaling the coming of winter.

Winter brought snows that were usually heavy, covering everything in sight. Power lines would sag and the trees would bend with the weight of the snow. Icicles would form on the cliffs and would be there until spring. Inside, everyone gathered around the stove to keep warm.

I have often thought that God provided

Mike and his sister, Susie

the beautiful blankets of snow to cover the bleakness of the coal camps that appeared after the spring and fall foliages disappeared.

Snow usually meant a vacation from school because the roads were steep and winding. It also meant a day for sledding. At night when the traffic slowed, we would go to the head of Chapman Fork and begin our ride on our sleighs. We built big fires to keep warm and even though the fast trip

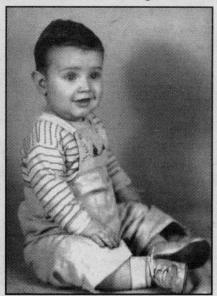

A very young Mike Sanders

down the mountain meant a 30-minute walk back up to repeat the ride, we did it over and over again.

Forbid them not... The children of Appalachia have grown to become some of the most talented people in this country. Our crafts are known worldwide, our authors have been recognized and we have produced leaders that have served in many different capacities. But, for each one that made it, there are thousands who did not. Today, life in the mountains is not much different from 40 years ago. There are so many children who make do with what they have; houses that are cold, not enough food or warm clothing, and no one to help them dream of a better tomorrow.

There is nothing more precious than our children; my own children and my grandchildren have enriched my life beyond measure. I am so proud of them, I am proud of the kind of people they have become and the lives they live. My moments with them can never be replaced. They are like the morning sun I enjoyed so much as a boy. They warm my life.

I really think dreaming set my feet on the path I'm on today. My dreams of traveling to other places led me to talk to an Army recruiter and years later, my dreams of helping people in an area where I grew up led me to begin working for the Christian Appalachian Project.

I've always encouraged my own kids to dream, and I want their kids to dream, too. I think if we encourage kids to dream, we also will be able to convince them that they can live those dreams, too.

And that's the worst burden that kids who live in poverty have to bear. Seldom do they have anyone tell them that they can and should dream. We hear about the "cycle of poverty," and that children who grow up in poverty don't know how to break out of that cycle. When we see families who have lived in the same substandard conditions for three generations, we can only conclude that that's true. At CAP, though, we think that the first step toward breaking that cycle of poverty begins with a dream.

Helping kids dream was one of the first programs that the Christian Appalachian Project started back in the 1950s. We didn't just say, "Come dream, kids." We made it look a whole lot better than that. We invited

Building lifelong friendships at CAP summer camps

them to camp, a small camp on Herrington Lake in Garrard County. It started small, with six kids, two counselors and a tarpaulin. All day, they would hike and swim and play games. At night, they would make a campfire and talk about their hopes and dreams. It wasn't easy at first. Lots of those kids had never even heard the question "What do you want to be when you grow up?" At Cliffview Lodge, though, they heard it over and over and eventually they started to dream. They dreamed of things they'd never dreamed before and the counselors helped them figure out how to make those dreams come true. Some of those boys dreamed about leaving the mountains to make their way in the world. Others, though, dreamed of ways that they could stay in the mountains, near their families, to make a difference for everyone around them.

We have two overnight camps — Camp Andrew Jackson and Camp Shawnee — and a day camp that give hundreds of kids from nearly two dozen counties in Eastern Kentucky and West Virginia that chance to dream.

Several years ago, we asked Jessica, a girl who had been to camp for many years to write some reflections of her years at camp. Through her, we learned just how influential our camps can be.

"If there is one lesson Camp AJ has taught me it is teamwork," Jessica wrote. "Whether you are on the adventure trail, orienting or just spotting on a difficult part of a hiking trail, teamwork is always involved. The teamwork I learned playing games as a seven-year-old camper helped me to learn survival skills as a 14 year-old. I learned that using your mind along with physical strength makes teamwork really work.

"I have gone to Camp Andrew Jackson for eight long years. Every year was better than the year before. My last year, I must say, was the best (but then, I can say that every year). I learned that experience and devotion really do pay off. I have also learned that Camp Andrew Jackson is part of me. If it were not for camp, I would not have such a warm love and ongoing determination in my personality. Thanks, Camp Andrew Jackson, for helping to mold me into who I am and who I will be. I, too, will always remember the little camp on the hill that is full of God's wonderful love."

After her years as a camper, Jessica came back to camp as a junior counselor and then as a counselor. Today, she's a remarkable young woman, one we're proud to call a "CAP Kid."

I know that the volunteers at both our camps work hard, staying up late and getting up early, working with kids that are sometimes hard to work with. But I guess there must be more to it than just hard work, because so many of them come back year after year. The contact with our volunteers is one of the most valuable parts of camp for the kids. The volunteers come from places all over the United States, and they tell the kids about the differences in other parts of the country. Some come from big cities, others from rural areas in the Midwest, we've even had volunteers from Alaska. In hearing stories about other places, kids can begin to dream about places they can go and things they can do. While we never like to encourage young people to move away from the mountains, we also don't want them to feel trapped into staying here because they don't know of opportunities that might be available in other places.

Several years after our camps were up and running successfully, we learned that one of the most effective ways to make sure children are successful in school is to make certain that they have been well prepared before they even start first grade. Even before the federal government began the Head Start program, CAP had initiated child development centers where kids beginning at the ages of three or four could come to learn their colors, numbers and ABCs. They learned how to play and share. They learned that school is fun. The most important lessons they learned, though taught them that God loves them and that they are valuable, worthwhile people. Over 25 years later, we have five centers and we're still teaching those lessons.

Some people might think that child development centers are nothing more than fancy baby-sitters, and if you're tempted to think along those lines, I'll invite you to step into one of our centers. They're bright, airy places, with plenty of window and color. They're divided into areas that encourage children to explore and experiment with science, art, reading, even housekeeping. They have great playgrounds because our teachers know how important it is that kids have a chance to play outside. The outside toys and equipment is designed for children to play together and to play safely.

There are always parents in the center, too, and that's one of the things I like the best. I see moms playing with all the kids, not just their own and while the parents are playing, they're also learning from the teachers. They're learning how to play with children on their level. They're learning important lessons about how to discipline children. We encourage parents to learn how to effectively discipline their children without spanking and we encourage children to "use their words" rather than their hands to settle differences. This teaches children other ways to deal with frustration without violence.

I've learned a lot about how important imagination is for children, and it makes me realize that, instinctively, CAP was right on target when it was encouraging children to dream many years ago.

Several of our centers now offer family literacy programs that enables parents — mostly moms, but some dads, too — an opportunity to work on their G.E.D. at the same time that their children are working on skills that will enable them to make a successful start in kindergarten.

Because we've been involved with child development for so many years, we've had the pleasure of seeing our child development students return to us at Teen Centers, which also give young people the opportunity to participate in community service projects.

Life is hard for teenagers everywhere, and in Appalachia it's no different. At CAP teen centers, we try to encourage kids to have fun and not grow up too fast. While they're having fun, we give them the opportunity to use the skills God has given them to serve their community. Many of those teens have also been involved in our teen leadership camps, where young people gather for a week of activities that will begin to equip them with the skills they need to influence the future of Appalachia.

Our children are the future for our country and we must take care of them. When I was young there was not a CAP, but I often wonder what it would have been like if there had been. We want kids to dream about the future because the best dreamers are the best leaders. I cannot begin to express the joy I have in being able to help make life a little better for our young. I am thankful each day for the many donors that support this organization and allow us to provide programs, camps or outreach that helps the children here in Appalachia.

A child from CAP's Child Development Center

CHAPTER VI

The silver-haired head is a crown of glory, if it be found in the way of righteousness.

Proverbs 16:31

People from the mountains have a special attachment to family. Remembering my mom and dad always brings a smile to my face when I think about all the life lessons they taught me. When they really wanted to make a point, they used words, but usually they didn't have to — I learned from their example. I really think they were the best parents anyone could ever have.

I find myself counting my blessings a lot these days — which I'm sure is true of most people who battle serious illness. My parents are among the greatest blessings I've had in 50-plus years of living. They taught me the importance of honesty and truth, the

Early coal chute in Majestic

importance of working hard and of loyalty. And they taught me to love God.

My dad, J.B., has retired from the coal mines. I don't think I've ever met anyone who worked harder than my dad. In his 30 years working in the deep mines, I can't remember that he ever missed one day's work. I remember seeing Dad and all the other miners trooping home, tired and dirty from a day underground. But he was never too tired to pick me up, when I was small enough to pick up, and when I got older, put an arm around my shoulder and ask about my day.

He and my mother, Patsy, still live in the same house where I grew up. My sister, Susie, still lives close by in Freeburn with her husband, Steve, and their children. Steve is more like a brother to me than an in-law.

I'm sorry to say I took a lot of my parents' love and support for granted when I was growing up. I just thought that's the way all families were. It wasn't until I got into the army and started to see a little bit of the world that I learned how special my folks, and later my in-laws, were and still are.

When I got older, I found out that not all parents worked and sacrificed the way mine did. I met guys in the army that hadn't talked to their brothers or sisters in months or even years. Somehow, they just didn't have the kind of ties to their folks that I had to mine.

There are many elderly in Appalachia who have entered the last portion of their lives alone; with not enough money for their medicines or the food they need each day. The loneliness that they endure causes many to die early or shrink away from society.

When I started working for CAP, I met people whose families ties were close, more like mine, but their children had moved away from the mountains to find work. The OPEC oil embargo of the 1970s had a "boom" effect on the mines. That several year period was followed by lay-offs and unemployment that forced people to move away from the mountains in search of jobs and other opportunities. Often they had to leave behind elderly parents and grandparents who depended on grown children for many things, including grocery shopping, transportation and just plain companionship. We've developed a program to give elderly people the assistance that most of them would get from their families, if those families hadn't had to move away to find work.

Elderly service workers say they never have a "typical" day, but schedule their time according to the needs the folks in their program have for transportation.

"Most of the time, when we get a referral from a doctor or a home health agency, it's for transportation," says Melissa Vance, a manager of CAP elderly services. "If they need transportation, that clues me in to something else. It's telling me that they probably don't have any family support."

In most counties we serve, other agencies provide services like cleaning and yard chores, shopping and personal services. But there are rarely enough resources to serve everyone with needs, and one of the biggest needs goes unmet. That's the need for simple friendship.

Naomi McIntosh, who works with elderly folks in Owsley County, says people are starved to death for somebody to talk to, so that's a lot of what our workers do — just sit and talk — in addition to driving folks to the doctor and helping them with shopping and chores. Owsley County, one of the poorest counties in the nation, is in an isolated area without many stores, so every so often Naomi loads her van with folks from her program and they take off for a somewhat larger town for groceries and doctor visits.

I think that the loneliness of some of our elderly friends is one of the great ironies of life in the 21st century. We have the longest life expectancy in history, but for many people, those additional years are filled with sorrow from being physically separated from family and loved ones, and pain that often accompanies advancing age. And there's another irony of the 21st century. Modern medicine has made remarkable advances in health care — in fact, I have some of those advances to thank in my cancer treatment. But for many people, those advances are so expensive that they are unaffordable, especially for people with inadequate insurance or no insurance at all.

Access, or lack of access, to medication is particularly troublesome. Medicare and Medicaid, health insurance that is provided to low-income people, does not include prescription coverage. Some medicines are affordable — fortunately, several antibiotics fall into that category. But medicines that are new to the market are often priced sky-high, and out of the reach of many of the people in our programs. I just have to shake my head when I realize that for many illnesses, cures are available — at the right price.

The Appalachian area also accounts for

some of the highest rates of diabetes and high blood pressure, and many of those with chronic illnesses are elderly people. Those illnesses can be controlled with medication, but those medicines must be taken exactly as they are prescribed. Many of our elderly in poverty can only afford to take half of the medicine prescribed, and even then they might have to choose between taking their medicine and paying the electric bill, or even buying food.

Several years ago, we learned that the large pharmaceutical companies in the United States were required to provide medication at no cost to needy patients. When our workers looked into the programs, they learned that every medication had different regulations for application; each must have a physician's signature and oversight, and must be requested every three months. The amount of paperwork is confusing at best, staggering at worst and practically impossible for people to complete.

We decided to take on prescription

Prescription Assistance Participant

assistance as part of our elderly services program, although people of all ages are eligible to participate. In the first year that CAP workers managed the paper-work, signatures and details of prescription assistance, we helped patients with over $600,000 worth of prescription medication. Within two years, that total had reached over $1 million, and during our last fiscal year, CAP workers accessed nearly $2.7 million in medications that would have otherwise been unaffordable to 2,838 people. This amounted to a savings of over $951.00 per person on prescription medication.

But as proud as I am of those numbers, and pleased to be able to help the elderly people in our program with medications, when I think of our elderly services, I am reminded of Dennis. Dennis passed away a few years ago, but due to his friendship with CAP, and a CAP volunteer in particular, his last years were happy and fulfilled.

I will always remember Dennis. Dennis was an elderly gentleman who lived in an old run down camper that was parked along the side of the road. He did not have running water or any type of bathroom. Bill, a volunteer with CAP had been made aware of Dennis' condition and began to work with him. Bill asked me to meet Dennis and witness first hand his condition. I did and realized that we had to do something to help.

Bill had grown very fond of Dennis through his work with him and wanted to do something special for him. He learned that his birthday was coming up, so he planned a party for him.

Dennis was alone, thus he was very

apprehensive when Bill asked him to go with him to a birthday party held in his honor. Bill had invited some of our elderly participants. Dennis agreed to go and seemed to be pleased. When Bill arrived to pick him up, he found that Dennis had run away to hide. The thoughts of a party made him afraid or embarrassed, because he had not had a birthday party in many, many years. Bill finally talked him into going. It was such a wonderful time for him. I will never forget the smile of pride and pleasure on his face. It was his moment in the sun.

We were able to get a local lady to give Dennis a small partial of land. Through our housing program and Operation Sharing, we were able to build Dennis a modest house to live out his life. It was a dream come true for him. He had electric lights and running water. He had enough space for the few treasures he had collected.

I will always remember his smile, his modest frail frame, and the dream that

CAP was able to make come true for him.

CAP's work with the elderly residents of Appalachia and the challenges they face has opened my heart and eyes. As my parents grow older and begin to need help, I'll try to be there for them when I can. I'm so thankful my sister lives close and takes such good care to help them out daily. My Dad has had to be in the hospital quite a bit this past year, and I want to spend every moment I can with him, whether it be taking him to the doctor, sitting in the hospital or just comforting my mom. They mean so much to me and I want them to know that they are loved.

I regret that we do not live closer to my Mother-in-law and Father-in-law. They have loved me like a son and are truly like parents to me. I have always felt welcomed in their home and often felt that I was treated as one of their own. They have always been very giving to all of us, especially during times of need. My wife's brothers and sister consider me as if I were a brother, and I think of them as my sister and brothers, and for that I am eternally grateful. This sense of family permeates my life and gives me great happiness and peace.

With each passing year I realize more and more that while our future lies within our youth, the lessons of our past and wealth of knowledge for tackling the future lies within our elderly. They are very precious assets that must be taken care of by all of us.

CAP's future is built upon the present, and we have been blessed with many people that help us each year. Certainly, many of these people identify with the area or the things we do to help people in need.

One of these people holds a special place in my heart because of the kind of person I have witnessed her to be and because of the trust she has bestowed upon our organization. Her name is Stella Parton, not only does she have a beautiful voice, but she also has a beautiful heart, one dedicated to doing the work of God. She works for God every day, and believes in the power of prayer. Upon first meeting her, I was touched with her genuine care and love for the people of Appalachia. I witnessed this concern through the tenderness she showed to an elderly lady and her family that we were helping in far eastern Kentucky. I witnessed it through her dedication to prayer and our Savior.

CAP donors are some of the most compassionate and caring people in America. Many have supported our programs for years and give from their hearts. This is not something we take lightly here at CAP. We know the donors have entrusted to us their resources to be used wisely. The donors expect, and rightfully so, that their gifts be used to help the most people we can in the best way we can.

Some of our donors get an opportunity to visit our operations and leave with a renewed understanding of what we do here in Appalachia. Their hearts are touched when they see the conditions our participants must endure, but their hope is revived as they observe our programs in action.

CAP has always used a philosophy of "teach a man to fish and he will feed himself." This requires a "hand-up" approach in our programs that help individuals and families break free of the suffocating bonds of poverty.

Majestic Church

I spend a lot of my time talking to donors or listening to their ideals. We share experiences and often times we pray together. As often as I can I write to them and sometimes have an opportunity to visit their homes. I have never failed to be amazed by the support and help people are willing to lend.

CAP has been so blessed to have so many people who want to help with God's work through the many programs we provide. It is on this support that CAP can help build better lives and a brighter future for those God has called us to serve.

Chapter VII

The Lord is on my side; I will not fear

Psalm 118:6

I believe that God watches out for every one of us in a special way. God's hand is in everything that happens to us and I deeply believe that everything happens for a reason.

The times I know that God has been watching out for me haven't always been that dramatic, but they're constant, nevertheless. Knowing that God is always there, always with me, has driven me to continue working as much as I could through the times that I've been going through chemo or some other type of treatment or therapy. Knowing that the work I do through CAP is helping the people of God has given me the energy to keep going. I know that God is looking out and taking care of me, so I'm going to look out for and take care of the things that he's entrusted to me.

I spent yesterday evening listening to the President of our country give his State of the Union Address. I listened to his plan for a better tomorrow and could not help but wonder about our people in Appalachia. Our country has been through a lot over the past two years. Terrorism, a soft economy, and rising health care cost have caused many to suffer as companies close their doors. All have placed a grip of fear on us. Many of these problems have faced the people of Appalachia all their lives. Today's conditions have presented heavy burdens for everyone, but they have become heavier for the nation's poor.

In 1960, John F. Kennedy saw first-hand the poverty in Appalachia as he passed through West Virginia and Kentucky during his bid to become president. It was Kennedy's initiatives that later became the

War on Poverty declared by then President Lyndon Johnson, illuminating the plight of thousands of men, women and children throughout the Appalachian region. President Johnson declared this war on poverty in a small county in eastern Kentucky, then one of the poorest regions in America.

Over the past decades this war against the conditions of poverty took the form of a relief program called welfare. In theory this was a noble effort of a nation caring for its poor and down trodden. However, in practice it became ineffective and many felt it did not address the root causes of poverty.

If you've ever been poor, or have gone without necessities for a period of time, you know how frightening that can be. Especially, if you have a family depending on you to provide for their basic needs and there is little or no work available, you suffer not just physically but emotionally as well. Many of those God has called us to serve lack confidence in their ability to provide for their families. Some have lost their sense of self-worth and believe they have nothing to offer. What is most discouraging is when we find those who have lost hope.

Over the years tremendous improvements have been made in the northern and southern counties of the Appalachian region. Stretching from New York down through Mississippi along the Appalachian Mountains, this rugged terrain has tremendous natural beauty and an abundance of natural resources. Highways have opened up much of the region to industry providing jobs and opportunities that had for so long eluded those who lived in the area. These developments have dramatically improved a large portion of lives in the northern and southern regions of Appalachia.

Yet, what once was a barrier to westward expansion of this nation's earliest explorers and settlers, the mountains in Central Appalachia have continued to create an area of isolation and hardship. Sixteen of the poorest counties in America are clustered in the eastern Kentucky coalfield region. It was in this region the War on Poverty began, and it is here the war continues to be fought.

As I look to the future I realize CAP will face many challenges in the years to come. Our work in Appalachia over the decades has shown us it will require more than just good intentions to make lasting changes that improve the quality of life for those who struggle in poverty. But, if I have learned one thing, it is that this organization has always been at the forefront in recognizing the needs of an area and it's people.

We have always had the flexibility and the capability of rising up to meet those needs. We do so by developing programs that provide care for our children and elderly, educational opportunities and job skill training for adults to become employable, and advocates within the communities

Too many homes are in disrepair

where we work to build partnerships with the local resources.

Over the past two years we have made decisions that will better position us in the heart of Appalachia, the area identified by the Appalachian Regional Commission as being the poorest in the country. It is our hope and prayer that we will be able to make more progress than ever before, by coming face to face with the poverty of the region and involving the communities and their people in finding solutions to their problems.

I believe that correctly identifying a

problem puts you halfway closer to solving it. However, many problems are not simple and become complex as they intertwine with other issues. Yet problems can be seen as challenges, or more importantly, opportunities.

This area of Appalachia we serve has a variety of problems, some from physical and geographical isolation, some from governmental neglect, and some from the lack of necessary infrastructure to attract industries that could provide jobs and the educational base needed to uplift the area.

To overcome a great deal of these problems, I envision us partnering more with local communities. We will need to help them find ways to improve the areas, thus, improving the lives of those who live within the community.

"Give a man a fish; you have fed him for today. Teach a man to fish; and you have fed him for a lifetime"
— Author unknown

I often use this saying when I talk about CAP's ministry. To me it is the wisdom we must practice as we serve those God has called us to serve with responsibility, accountability, and dignity. We must be the teachers that promote learning and instill a hunger for knowledge. We must teach the people and the communities how to "fish".

CAP has been teaching in Appalachia for many years. Our human-service programs reach out to those in need with compassion and God's love, not in pity but rather with understanding and hope. Our programs promote not just short-term crisis intervention but long-term development of the person or family as well. We refer to this as giving "a hand up — not a hand out". By doing it in this way we do not promote dependency, we require involvement of that person or family to the extent possible.

What makes CAP programs different than so many others? I believe there are several differences. First, our programs have long-term development as a goal. We measure this achievement based on positive changes in the conditions and quality of life of our participants. Second, CAP programs respect the dignity of those we serve. We will not exploit our participants or compromise their privacy or confidentiality. Lastly, our programs are built on relationships. It is the human touch that ultimately makes the difference — compassion and genuine caring for that person we are serving. Our participants are not numbers to us — they're faces with names. When they cry we cry; when they rejoice we rejoice as well.

More and more CAP will be working in these communities to build a coalition of partnerships with local resources. Our goal here is to develop effective working relationships that serve both the community and their citizens in need. CAP can bring to this coalition a tremendous amount of resources that includes manpower, experience, Operation Sharing gifts-in-kind, proven programs, integrity, compassion and Christian love.

I just recently read where prescription drug abuse had reached epidemic levels in eastern Kentucky, Tennessee and West Virginia. With drug abuse not only does the abuser suffer, but there are many victims: children, parents, grandparents and the community. Victims not able to pick up the pieces of their lives without help. This is a relatively new challenge for Central Appalachia and places additional weight on those already suffocating from poverty. It is a problem that will require action, education

Children love to learn at CAP's
Child and Family Development centers

and prayer to defeat.

While every day will present its own challenges, I think if we stay focused on the family and family values, we work hard and serve God and not ourselves, we will continue this mission to serve those God has called us to serve..

We are able to do these things because we have a great ministry, one that is made up of many hearts: donors and volunteers from all over the country, CAP employees, and countless others who have joined hands to make a better tomorrow for the people of Appalachia.

We open our doors to our donors and invite them to come and see first-hand what their prayers and support means to the people of this area.

Each year I write and send many letters of request to many people who help us. This work excites me and I want to give an invitation to as many people as I can to share in this ministry. Each year we are blessed by the response of our donors — they always come through with the prayers and financial support crucial for our programs to continue. I appreciate greatly this support and pray daily God will use every ounce of my being in this ministry. My heart and soul are in this work; I love every day I enter the doors of the Christian Appalachian Project. This ministry has given my life great meaning and a profound sense of peace.

I have been blessed the past two years with much goodness: my bout with cancer has helped me to see life differently, to appreciate all that is holy and to be ever mindful of our Savior's wishes for us while on His earth. As a result, I have written down 10 things that I would like to share with others. These small adjustments have helped to make my life better than it has ever been.

1. I take less for granted
2. I encourage others toward cancer preventative measures
3. My family has become closer
4. My faith in God has strengthened
5. I am a happier person than ever before
6. I look at things like I never looked at them before
7. I realize how short and precious life is
8. I appreciate my faith and my church more
9. I've wanted to do more to help people than ever before
10. God has shown me that there is nothing to fear.

If I could offer advice to my family, especially my children, their wonderful spouses, and grandchildren, my friends and all those I hold dear, I would say to them, "Love those around you, and do not make enemies. Love God first, make your church a center point of your life. Draw your strength and courage from the word of the Lord. Spend the rest of your life helping others. For our Lord said it best, whatever you do for the least of my brethren — you do for me."

I see the work we're doing here on earth as preparation for the home that God is preparing for us in heaven, and when He calls me home; I'll be ready and willing to go. We spend our growing-up years listening to God's word through the Bible, and those words have taught me that when we leave this place on earth, God promised us a much better and glorious place.

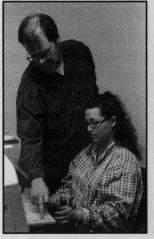

As we head into the future, CAP will continue to focus on our mission and our guiding principles for our daily direction:

Hard at work at CAP's Adult Learning center

CAP Mission Statement

The Christian Appalachian Project is an interdenominational, non-profit Christian organization committed to serving people in need in Appalachia by providing physical, spiritual and emotional support through a wide variety of programs and services.

Our Guiding Principles

1. To promote the dignity and self-worth of individuals by promoting self help.

2. To practice and encourage good stewardship of and accountability for all of the resources entrusted to us.

3. To foster individual growth among staff, volunteers, donors and program participants.

4. To live out and promote the Gospel through all our actions.

5. To foster open, honest and effective communication both inside and outside the organization.

6. To involve the Appalachian people of all social and economic levels in developing solutions to poverty.

My life has been a gift from God, and I hope that through my work at CAP, helping His children, my life has been a gift to Him. As I have served, I've had the opportunity to learn so much about the really important things in life. I am looking forward to what lies ahead.

I may not know what the future holds, but I know whose hand holds the future.

"Trust in God, it's in his hands"

A special thank you...

The integrity of our organization is without question. We are who we are today because of all the people who have been and are still involved in our work. For this I want to say "thank you to each one."

To our management staff for support and leadership; the employees and volunteers for their dedication and commitment; our Board of Directors for their guidance and the giving of their time to help others; Monsignor Ralph Beiting for starting the Christian Appalachian Project and for having the strength and vision to dream as a young man; to my family for sacrificing their time with me to allow me to serve God's people. I want to thank our supporters that help us financially and pray for us in carrying out this wonderful ministry. Most of all I want to thank God for the challenges He has given me, my development in life, His preparing me for what I do and for His guidance in the work we do each day.

God bless you all.
Mike Sanders

Angels of Appalachia

Please consider joining this special committed group of individuals who support the Christian Appalachian Project through monthly or quarterly gifts.

As part of this honored group, you will receive periodic updates about CAP's work in Appalachia. In addition, you will receive an Angel Pin signifying to the world your commitment to our programs. Finally, your name will be inscribed on our Honor Roll.

If you would like to join us, please complete the order form below.

Name_____

Address_____

City_____State____ Zip_____

E-mail Address_____

Mail this form to: Angels of Appalachia, Christian Appalachian Project, Development Office, P.O. Box 511, Lancaster KY 40444-0511.

1-866-270-4227

The Mountain Spirit

Our quarterly magazine The Mountain Spirit, will keep you up-to-date on the work of the Christian Appalachian Project as we continue to help the people of this poverty-stricken area help themselves. In the magazine, you will also find moving, inspiring stories about the people we serve. If you would like to subscribe to this publication, or request a free sample, please complete the order form below.

THE MOUNTAIN SPIRIT
Subscription Order Form

❑ Please send me CAP's magazine *The Mountain Spirit*. Subscription rate: One year – $8.00.

Name_____

Address_____

City_____State____ Zip_____

E-mail Address_____

As our founder, one of Father Beiting's dreams was to personally share the vision of CAP with you and your church or civic group. For more information on available dates for a CAP representative to speak with your group, please contact our Major Gifts and Planned Giving Office, at Christian Appalachian Project, P.O. Box 511, Lancaster, KY 40444-0511, or call (859) 792-3051 www.chrisapp.org

Dear Mike Sanders,

❏ I am interested in helping to fulfill your dreams for Appalachia. Please contact me in reference to planned and major giving opprotunities.

❏ Please contact me to arrange for a visit from a CAP representative to your area.

❏ Please send me free literature about making planned gifts/charitable gift annuities, or including CAP in my estate planning.

❏ Please send me information about CAP's endowment fund.

Name _____

Address _____

City _____State____ Zip_____

E-mail Address _____

Mail this form to: Major Gifts and Planned Giving, Christian Appalachian Project, Development Office, P.O. Box 511, Lancaster KY 40444-0511.

I am interested in volunteering with the Christian Appalachian Project

Please send me information on:

❑ One-year volunteer opportunities
(year round admissions)

❑ Summer Camp volunteer opportunities
(June - August)

❑ Short-term volunteer opportunities

❑ Group opportunities

Please return this form to and/or contact us at:

Name_____

Address_____

City_____State____Zip_____

E-mail Address_____

Christian Appalachian Project
Volunteer Recruitment
6550 South Ky. Rt. 321
P. O. Box 459
Hagerhill, KY 41222
E-mail: volunteer@chrisapp.org.
or call 1-800-755-5322